Green Bay's

13

Championship
Seasons

Jim Rice

Author

This is Jim Rice's fourth book. He is a former history teacher and school superintendent who now writes about sports history. For his other books, visit giantcheeseheads.com

92 Years!
Bears-Packers 1921-2013
(Includes 2014)

Great Games of the Gridiron
NFL Championship Games 1933-1965

Giant Cheeseheads!
The Giant-Packer Rivalry 1928-2014

2016 Giant Cheesehead Books
giantcheeseheads.com

Editor: Bill Mayer

ISBN: 1530417090
ISBN: 13:9781530417094

Green Bay's **13** Championship Seasons

"There are teams that evoke something beyond merely winning and losing. Celtics. Yankees. Notre Dame. The Packers are such a team."

Tim Layden
Sports Illustrated
2/14/2011

The Winning Tradition

The winning tradition of the Green Bay Packers is unsurpassed. They have won more NFL championships than any other team, and the franchise has become synonymous with excellence since their first title in 1929. The Packers followed that first championship with two more to become the first team in the history of the young league to win three straight NFL titles. In the three year period, their record was 34-5-3, and they outscored opponents 723-220!

In 1933, the NFL divided teams into two divisions. Division winners began playing for the league championship. This new NFL Championship Game crowned pro football's champion from 1933-1965. The Packers played in this game for the first time in 1936, and overall they made eight appearances, winning six.

With the merger of the National Football League and the American Football League in 1966, the Super Bowl replaced the NFL Championship Game as pro football's top prize. In the 50 years since, the Packers have won four Super Bowls - I, II, XXXI, and XLV. They are the most recent examples of the excellence that has produced 13 championships for Green Bay, and made the community-owned Packers one of the most endearing franchises in professional sports.

The Lambeau Dynasty
1921 – 1949   212-106-21 (68%)
6 Championships

Earl "Curly" Lambeau <u>was</u> the Green Bay Packers. He founded the team with the help of his employer, the local newspaper, and the football fans of northeastern Wisconsin. A former football star at Green Bay East High School, Lambeau was well known in the area, and his athletic reputation attracted players for the team.

From 1919 to 1949, Lambeau led the Packer franchise. He played until 1929 when he retired to concentrate on coaching, selecting players, signing contracts and promoting the team. His vision and leadership helped steer the team and pro football toward unimagined success.

When the Packers joined a professional league in 1921, some thought it would never compete with college football. Many of the locals wondered if there was enough interest in football beyond a few hours of college football on Saturday afternoon. Lambeau believed there was, and he also knew that a professional league would help develop the game of football further, and increase its overall popularity. He was right.

Lambeau led Green Bay for 31 years. His belief in the forward pass put Green Bay on the cutting edge, and it laid a permanent foundation for successful team. After he departed, the Packers did not have another winning season for ten years.

1929 12-0-1
Offense # 2
Defense # 1

The Packers finished fourth in 1928, and Curly Lambeau made several off-season moves to strengthen the roster. Cal Hubbard, Johnny "Blood" McNally, and Mike Michalski were acquired, and they transformed a good team into a great one. Their dominating defense gave up 22 points all season. They didn't allow a touchdown until the sixth game, and they recorded eight shut outs.

The Chicago Cardinals scored that first touchdown, but when they missed the extra point the Packers won 7-6. Green Bay outscored its next three opponents 42-6, and November's rematch with the Cardinals marked Lambeau's last game as a player.

The only blemish on their record in 1929 was a tie in Game 10. After winning one of the biggest games in league history the week before (below), they fell flat the next week with a 0-0 tie against Frankford. Fortunately, they still finished ahead of the Giants (13-1-1).

⟫ Key Game 11/24/29
Packers @ Giants   Polo Grounds 25,000

Less than one month after the Great Stock Market Crash of 1929, the Packers met the Giants in a de facto championship game. A battle between these two undefeated powers attracted nationwide attention.

Ironically, the Packers were the bigger and more physical team, and according to the *New York Telegram*, they made the Giants look, "like pygmies."[1] When the Giants fumbled on their first possession, Johnny Blood scooped it up and the Packers scored a few plays later. The rain and Vern Lewellen's long punts kept New York deep in its own territory for most of the first half.

In the third quarter, Giant quarterback Bennie Friedman completed three straight passes to get them into the end zone. He missed the extra point and Green Bay was still in front. The fourth quarter was all Packers. Their offensive line pushed the Giants around, and they chewed up the clock with two long touchdown drives. Bo Molenda led the strong running game on both drives. He scored the first touchdown, which turned out to be the winner, and Johnny Blood delivered the second score to put the game out of reach.

Ten men played the entire game for Green Bay! Art Daley of the New York Times was impressed, and he praised the visitors, "The hard running, hard fighting Green Bay Packers punctured the bubbles of the Giants invincibility Sunday by tramping roughshod over the hitherto unbeaten New Yorkers."[2] The win gave Green Bay the inside track for the championship with three games remaining.

Packers	7	0	0	13	20
Giants	0	0	6	0	6

1930 10-3-1
Offense # 2
Defense # 4

Green Bay's second championship team was an outstanding one. While not as dominant as the first, this squad was a fine team. Eleven new players meshed seamlessly with the veterans, and the most notable newcomer, Arnie Herber, became the first great Packer quarterback who specialized in throwing the long pass. Herber was the first 1,000 yard passer, and he was fortunate to play for Curly Lambeau, "the most pass oriented coach in the NFL."[3]

Green Bay began the season with eight straight wins to extend their undefeated streak to 23 games! Four of the wins were shutouts. The streak ended in November with back-to-back losses to the Chicago Cardinals and the New York Giants. In both games, two stars – Fullback Ernie Nevers of the Cardinals and Quarterback Benny Friedman of the Giants – threw for one touchdown, ran for another, and kicked the extra point! The Packers lost both 13-6.

After they beat Frankford and Staten Island, Green Bay finished with a loss to the Bears, and a tie against the Portsmouth Spartans. The tie against Portsmouth clinched the title for the Packers who finished 10-3-1 (.769), just ahead of the New York Giants (13-4-0/.765).

⟫ <u>Key Game</u> 12/14/30
Packers @ Spartans Universal Stadium 4,500

A first quarter touchdown pass from Red Dunn saved the Packer season. But when Dunn missed the extra point, it cost them the game!

In the first quarter, the Packers took over at their 45 yard line and drove to the Portsmouth 15. On fourth down, they gambled with a pass play. Dunn threw to Wuert Engelmann for the touchdown, but Dunn surprisingly missed the extra point.

Portsmouth came right back, successfully running the ball through the Packer defense. They scored an apparent touchdown on a pass from Father Lumpkin to Red Joseph, but it was ruled out of bounds. The Spartans finally tied it in the second quarter when they used a series of "spinners, reverses, straight smashes and end runs to put the ball over."4 The important extra point though went wide for a 6-6 first half.

Green Bay did little offensively after scoring early. Portsmouth held the upper hand for most of the third quarter, but they could not put up any points. In the final quarter, interceptions by Green Bay's Lavvie Dilweg and Johnny Blood stopped two late threats by the Spartans.

Packers	6	0	0	6
Spartans	0	6	0	6

1931 12-2-0
Offense # 1
Defense # 2

For the third straight year, the Packers were king. Even with 13 new players on the roster, the offense was nearly unstoppable. The 48 points they scored against Providence were the most ever scored by a Packer team to that point. For the season, they scored 116 more points than anyone else!

With a stout defense that recorded five shutouts, the Packers won their first nine games. The Chicago Cardinals snapped the steak in November as Ernie Nevers threw two touchdown passes in a 21-13 victory. The Packers won their next three contests before bowing to the Bears to end the season.

Green Bay finished one game ahead of Portsmouth to win the title, but it was not without controversy. The 1931 schedule had not included a game between Green Bay and Portsmouth. When they finished in first and second place respectively, the Spartans claimed that the Packers had agreed to play a game against them. Green Bay denied doing so, and Portsmouth appealed to Commissioner Joe Carr, who sided with Green Bay.

▶ <u>Key Game</u> 10/25/31
Steam Roller @ Packers City Stadium 6,000

A *Homecoming Game* for Green Bay brought back many retired stars. The honor roll included Cub Buck, Eddie Kotal, Charlie Mathys and Red Smith. The current squad rose to the occasion, and put on an impressive show.

In the first six minutes, Green Bay's Wuert Englemann caught two touchdown passes from Red Dunn. Later in the quarter, he returned a kickoff 85 yards for a 21-0 Packer lead!

Green Bay had trouble containing Providence's passing game when it came alive in the third quarter. Former Packer Oran Pape, who ran for a touchdown in the first half, caught two touchdown passes bring Providence to within eight. The Packers answered swiftly, and they dominated the fourth quarter with three touchdowns. Fullback Bo Molenda ran for a touchdown, and he threw 40 yards to Roger Grove for the other score to wrap up the win.

Steam Roller	0	7	13	0	20
Packers	21	7	0	20	48

1936 10-1-1
Offense # 1
Defense # 4

In 1933, the NFL divided teams into the Eastern and Western Divisions. Division winners played for the championship, and the Packers made their first appearance in this game in 1936.

Green Bay was a preseason favorite. They had the league's best passing game with Arnie Herber and Don Hutson. Herber led the NFL in passing for the third time, and he became the first quarterback to pass for more than 1,000 yards. Hutson led the league with eight touchdown catches.

As was the custom until the 1970s, the Packers opened the season with home games and then finished the year on the road. Their only loss came in the second game when the Bears' powerful offense pummeled them 30-3. After the loss, Lambeau agreed to the salary demands of holdout Johnny Blood.

The Packers won their next nine games. The victories included a bounce back win over the Bears, and two wins over the Redskins. After clinching the Western Division, they played to a 0-0 tie against the Cardinals.

❯ NFL Championship Game 12/13/36
Packers vs. Redskins   Polo Grounds   29,545

The game was played in sunny New York City when Redskins owner George Preston Marshall moved the game out of Boston because of his dislike of the fans there. He would relocate his team to Washington D.C. in 1937, and he hoped to bring along the 1936 NFL Championship.

The Packers though were, "billed as the greatest forward passing team that ever invaded New York."5 They passed the ball more than any team, and they had the top offense. Boston had a strong defense, but they were stronger against the run than the pass.

In the first minutes, the Redskins fumbled at midfield. Packer quarterback Arnie Herber connected with Don Hutson in stride 30 yards away for a stunning 48-yard touchdown. Boston got six back on the first play of the second quarter, but they missed the extra point to trail 7-6.

The Redskins had lost star running back, Cliff Battles, on the tenth play of the game. His loss crippled their offense, and they were held scoreless in the second half. The Packers continued to ride the arm of Arnie Herber. Early in the third quarter, he launched a towering 52-yard pass to Johnny Blood. Blood made a spectacular catch to put the ball at the Redskin eight. Boston then covered Blood and Hutson so closely, that Milt Gantenbein was wide open for six.

After blocking a punt, Green Bay scored again to put the game away. The Redskins were unable to generate a first down the entire second half, and the Packers proved once and for all that they could compete with the big city teams in the biggest city of all!

Packers	7	0	7	7	21
Redskins	0	6	0	0	6

1939 9-2-0
Offense # 3
Defense # 4

The 1930s closed with the Packers having the best quarterback duo in the league with veteran Arnie Herber and second-year man Cecil Isbell. They threw the most passes in the league, and their explosive offense was balanced. With Don Hutson catching passes and Clarke Hinkle running over opponents, Green Bay scored 13 touchdowns through the air and 14 on the ground. Hutson, the game's premier receiver, averaged 24.9 yards per catch which is still a Green Bay record!

The Packers beat both Chicago teams to start the season. After the Cleveland Rams rallied to defeat them, the Packers won seven of their next eight. Their only loss came in their rematch with the Bears. They finished the season with four straight wins, and the defense stiffened allowing just 29 points in the final four games.

The division title came down to the last game in Detroit. On a muddy field, Green Bay fell behind 7-3 in the first half. In the third quarter, they blocked a Lions punt out of the end zone for a safety. Later in the quarter on fourth down, Clarke Hinkle took it in over left tackle to put the Packers in front 12 7. That was all the Packers needed as the Lions never got beyond their own 35 yard line in the second half.

▶▶ NFL Championship Game 12/10/39
Giants @ Packers   State Fair Park   32,278

In an obvious financial move, the NFL moved the championship game *from* Green Bay to a venue with 8,000 more seats on the west side of Milwaukee. On a cold and windy day a la Green Bay, the Packers had a score to settle with the Giants who had beaten them in a brutal title game in 1938. Though the Packers were favored, the Giants hoped to become the first team in history to win two straight title games. They had the best record (9-1-1), the best defense, and they were confident.

A few days before the game, the mother of Giant coach Steve Owen passed away. Assistant Coach Bo Molenda, a former Packer, led the Giants in Owen's absence.

Strong winds and 35mph gusts kept both teams pretty quiet in the first half. The wind also shook the wooden press box, and many reporters feared it would be blown down! In the first half, the Giants picked-off three passes, but they missed on three field goals. Though they had one of the league's best running games, the Giants had trouble running without injured leading rusher Bill Paschal. The Packers scored the only points of the half when the Giants used three men to cover Don Hutson leaving Milt Gantenbein open over the middle for a Arnie Herber touchdown pass.

Green Bay took control of the game in the second half. Cecil Isbell, just as he was blasted by John Mellus of the Giants, uncorked a spectacular 31-yard pass to Joe Laws for a touchdown. It put the Packers up 17-0. Both Isbell and

Herber now had a touchdown pass, not a good sign for the Giants.

Green Bay's defense stopped New York at every turn. Six interceptions, two by rookie Charlie Brock, helped to deliver the first shutout in NFL Championship Game history. A proud Lambeau boasted, "There wasn't a team in the world that could beat our club today."[6]

The Packers repaid the Giants for 1938, and won their fourth NFL championship of the decade. After the game, when reporters asked New York owner Tim Mara about losing to Green Bay, Mara responded, "If we had to lose, there is no team I would rather lose to..."[7]

Giants	0	0	0	0	0
Packers	7	0	10	10	27

1944 8-2-0
Offense # 3
Defense # 4

Over 600 NFL players and coaches served their country during World War II. The quality of play was not as strong during the war. Many former players and retirees returned to the gridiron to fill out rosters and keep up the interest of the fans.

The Packers opened the season in Milwaukee by defeating the Brooklyn Tigers. They went on to win six straight including a 42-28 win over the Bears. With Hutson still the league's best receiver, they outscored opponents 161-69 during the streak.

After Game 6, the offense began to sputter. They were shut out by the Bears and the Giants. In New York, they lost to former Packer quarterback, Arnie Herber, and their former assistant coach, Red Smith. To make matters worse, after the 24-0 loss, Lambeau claimed the Giants had spied on Packer practices. Accusations went back and forth in the newspapers, but nothing was proven. The more likely scenario is that two former Packers, who had axes to grind with Lambeau, shared everything they knew about Green Bay and then some!

The Packers finished ahead of the second place Bears, and they outscored opponents 238-141. The Giants finished their season with four straight wins, including three shut outs.

⟫ NFL Championship Game 12/17/44
Packers @ Giants   Polo Grounds   46,016

The fervor surrounding November's game had settled down by the time they played for the title a month later. This was the third time in six years that Green Bay and New York battled for NFL supremacy!

The first quarter was a stalemate. The Packers didn't allow a first down, and the Giants punted seven times. In the second quarter, a hometown hero emerged for Green Bay.

Fullback Ted Fritsch of Spooner, Wisconsin broke the back of the top-ranked Giant defense with two touchdowns. After a powerful 23-yard dash over right tackle a few plays earlier, Fritsch took it in from the one. Later in the quarter, while three Giants followed Don Hutson, Fritsch was left wide open for a touchdown pass from quarterback Irv Comp.

The Giants never got beyond the 35-yard line in the first half. Packer cornerback Joe Laws kept the pressure on in the second half with two of his three interceptions. Laws also led the Packers in rushing with 74 yards.

The Giants scored in the final quarter when Arnie Herber marched them downfield. After Ward Cuff scored and narrowed it to seven with several minutes remaining, two of New York's final three drives ended in interceptions. "Everything worked to perfection"[8] Lambeau said afterwards. Though he coached the Packers for another five years, this was his sixth and final championship.

Packers	0	14	0	0	14
Giants	0	0	0	7	7

The Lombardi Dynasty
1959 – 1967   98-30-4 (77%)
5 Championships

Green Bay's climb to the top under Vince Lombardi was meteoric. In his second year, the Packers made it to the championship game losing to Norm Van Brocklin and the Philadelphia Eagles. In 1961, they reached the title game again this time facing Lombardi's former team the New York *Football* Giants.

Lombardi knew what a formidable opponent the Giants would be. They had the NFL's #1 offense and #2 defense. His Packers were no slouch coming in at #2 on offense and #1 on defense. No one could have anticipated the 37-0 blowout by the Packers. It was the first shut out of the Giants since 1953.

The Packers and Giants met again for the title in 1962. The game was closer, but Green Bay prevailed again 16-7. The 1961-62 Packers took the first steps of The Lombardi Dynasty. After defeating the Giants twice, Green Bay won three straight championships from 1965-67 to give Lombardi five championships in seven years.

1961 11-3-0
Offense # 1
Defense # 2

The Packers had not won a championship since 1944. After losing to the Eagles in the 1960 title game, they were determined to return and win. The schedule expanded from 12 to 14 games in 1961, and the Packers were favored to repeat in the Western Division.

The opener did not go as planned with a 17-13 loss to the Lions in Milwaukee. The Packers won their next six games with a potent offense that averaged 34 points per game. The winning streak ended in Baltimore, and so did Jerry Kramer's season when he broke his ankle.

The Packers paid back the Lions, and then met the Giants in Milwaukee. Both teams were 9-2, and a close game turned on a fourth quarter fumble and Jim Taylor's second touchdown of the day. Taylor also set a club record at the time with 186 yards rushing. The Packers split their final two games of the season to finish with the best record in the league. They waited confidently for the Giants.

⟫ <u>NFL Championship Game</u> 1 2/31/61
Giants @ Packers   City Stadium   39,029

"It was big ol' New York versus lil' Green Bay"₉ for the first championship game ever played in Green Bay. Before the game, fans christened their city *Titletown USA*, and near zero degree wind chills did little to dampen their enthusiasm. Surprisingly, Green Bay had little trouble with the Giants. Thanks to President Kennedy, Lombardi's friend, a weekend leave from the Army Reserve was arranged for Paul Hornung so he could play in the game. Hornung not only played, but he set a title game record with 19 points!

After a quiet first quarter, the Packers hit the Giants with a barrage of points. Paul Hornung started the scoring with a six yard run off right tackle. Bart Starr followed with touchdown passes to Boyd Dowler and Ron Kramer.

The Giants couldn't keep up. The Packers teed off on Giant quarterback Y.A. Tittle sacking him twice and intercepting four passes. Charlie Conerly, in the last game of his career, replaced Tittle in the second quarter. He lit a brief spark under the Giants, but his initial drive bogged down at the Packer six yard line. Green Bay took over on downs, and marched downfield for another Hornung field goal.

In the third quarter, a ray of hope appeared for New York when they forced the Packers to punt twice in succession. They couldn't capitalize though, and Tittle's return made little difference as the Giant offense got into Packer territory just twice all day. Green Bay's performance had Lombardi beaming and proclaiming, "Today, this was the greatest team in the history of the National Football League."[10] Starr's three touchdown passes led an offense that scorched the NFL's top-ranked defense. The Packers left no doubt that Green Bay was, indeed, Titletown USA!

Giants	0	0	0	0	0
Packers	0	24	10	3	37

1962 13-1-0
Offense # 1
Defense # 1

Green Bay was the clear favorite in 1962. They obliged by getting off to a lightning fast start with 10 straight wins thanks to quarterback, Bart Starr. It began with a 34-7 whipping of the Vikings followed by back-to-back shutouts of the Cardinals and Bears. The 49-0 defeat of the Bears was the biggest blowout in the rivalry's history. Detroit's strong defense then held Green Bay without a touchdown, but they couldn't stop Paul Hornung's kicking. The *Golden Boy* booted three field goals for a 9-7 win!

Despite a knee injury to Hornung, Green Bay annihilated their next five opponents by a combined score of 183-47. When they shutout the last place Eagles 49-0, they set a franchise record with 628 total yards. But any dreams of an undefeated season ended on Thanksgiving Day in Detroit. The Packers didn't score until the fourth quarter, and they were outgained by nearly 200 yards. The Lions sacked Starr 10 times, and they rolled 26-14.

Green Bay won its last three games to clinch the Western Division for the third straight year. In 1962, most teams were overmatched by Green Bay. They outscored opponents 415-148, and this group ranks with the very best teams in Packer history.

⟫ NFL Championship Game 12/30/62
Packers @ Giants   Yankee Stadium   64,892

A rematch with the Packers was just what the Giants wanted. They thought their loss in last year's title game was a fluke, and they couldn't wait to prove it. The Packers were ready for the rematch with an offense that had scored the second most points in NFL history!

In weather conditions that Lombardi described years later as worse than the Ice Bowl, it felt more like Green Bay than New York City. Wind gusts as strong as 40 mph played havoc with the passing game of both teams. "It shook my confidence"[11] Tittle admitted after the game, but he still threw for 197 yards.

Green Bay's top backfield of Jim Taylor, Paul Hornung and Tom Moore kept the offense moving. They ran 46 times for 148 yards. Taylor won his battle with Giant linebacker, Sam Huff, with 85 yards on 31 carries. He scored the game's only offensive touchdown, and with Jerry Kramer's three field goals, it was all the Packers needed.

For the second consecutive championship game, the Packers held New York's explosive offense scoreless. The only points they scored came on a blocked punt by Erich Barnes that was recovered in the end zone. It cut the lead to 10-7.

After the blocked punt, the Giants forced the Packers to punt on their next possession. Sam Horner fumbled the kick though, and it was recovered by Ray Nitschke. Kramer kicked his second field goal five plays later

Kramer added a third field goal in the fourth quarter to give Green Bay a nine point lead. Sensing victory, teammates mobbed Kramer near the sideline. Nitschke, who recovered two fumble recoveries and deflected a pass that was intercepted by Dan Currie, was the game's MVP. The win made it back-to-back titles for Lombardi's Packers.

Packers 3 7 3 3   16
Giants 0 0 7 0   7

1965 10-3-1
Offense # 8
Defense # 1

After a three year absence, the Green Bay returned to the championship game behind an outstanding defense. Before the title game, however, Green Bay played in the first overtime postseason game since 1958 when the Colts defeated the Giants.

In 1965, the Packers won their first six games. They beat both the Bears and the Lions in their first meeting, but later in the season they lost to them both. They beat the last place Rams 6-3, but lost to them in the rematch as well two weeks later.

Green Bay trailed the Colts by a half game in the Western Division when they met in Baltimore in Game 11. Paul Hornung's five touchdowns led to a resounding 42-27 Packer victory. But they failed to clinch the division the next week when they couldn't stop the 49ers game-tying drive. The 24-24 stalemate caused a tie atop the Western Division.

⫸ Western Conference Playoff 12/26/65
Colts @ Packers   Lambeau Field   50,484

Packers beat the Colts twice during the season, but both teams finished 10-3-1. This playoff game quickly became a battle of back-up quarterbacks. Baltimore's Johnny Unitas and back-up Gary Cuozzo were already out with injuries. Halfback Tom Matte was Baltimore's third string quarterback, and since he hadn't played the position since 1960 he taped the game plan to his wrist!

Packer quarterback Bart Starr was injured on the first play from scrimmage. He hurt his ribs by trying to tackle Don Shinnick who had recovered a Packer fumble. Veteran backup Zeke Bratkowski came in for Starr. After Shinnick scored on the early turnover, Lou Michaels gave the Colts a 10-0 lead with a field goal.

Baltimore went scoreless the rest of the way. The offense battled back with Bratkowski's 248 yards passing leading the way. A one-yard touchdown run by Paul Hornung, and a widely contested field goal by Don Chandler, forced the overtime. In the extra period, the Colts had the ball first. A bad snap foiled their field goal attempt from the 47-yard line. The Packers then drove to the Colt 25 yard line where Chandler kicked the uncontested winner 13 minutes into overtime.

Colts	7	3	0	0	0	10
Packers	0	0	7	3	3	13

⟫ NFL Championship Game 1/2/66
Browns @ Packers   Lambeau Field   50,777

In the last NFL Championship Game *before* the Super Bowl Era, the Packers faced the defending champion Cleveland Browns in what would turn out to be Jim Browns' last game.

Throughout its history, NFL Championship Game had been marred by bad, sometimes extreme weather. In this final game, nearly all of the elements made a final appearance: snow, rain, freezing rain, ice, fog and mud. It forced officials to place flags along the sidelines every 10 yards.

But the conditions had little effect on the Packers. Fans cheered the healthy return of Bart Starr, Paul Hornung and several others. Back from his rib injury, Starr struck early. On their first possession, though he slipped as he threw, Starr connected with Carroll Dale for a 47-yard touchdown.

Cleveland answered quickly with quarterback Frank Ryan completing passes to Jim Brown, Paul Warfield, and his big flanker back, Gary Collins. He eventually found Collins for the touchdown in the corner of the end zone. Cleveland missed the extra point, and after trading four field goals, the Packers led at intermission 13-12.

The second half was all Green Bay, and the opening drive was one for the ages. The power and precision of the Packer running game was on full display when Jim Taylor and Paul Hornung led an 11 play 90 yard touchdown drive that stretched the lead to 20-12.

The defense took it from there, blanking Cleveland in the second half. They completely dominated the trenches, held Jim Brown to 50 yards rushing, and gave up just 161 total yards. The Packers were back!

Browns 9 3 0 0 12
Packers 7 6 7 3 23

1966 12-2-0
Offense # 4
Defense # 1

One of the greatest teams in Packer history had the privilege representing the NFL in the first championship game against the American Football League. The new AFL-NFL World Championship Game was formally renamed the Super Bowl in 1968 .

The defending champions opened against their 1965 playoff opponents - the Colts and the Browns. Green Bay beat them both again, but against Cleveland they needed a touchdown in the final minutes to pull it out. The Packers won five of their next six before losing to Minnesota at home. They repaid the Vikings two weeks later.

In the last five games, the Packers' top ranked defense held opponents under two touchdowns per game. Despite Bart Starr's injury, they clinched the Western Conference in a gratifying 14-10 win in Baltimore. In the game's final minutes and the Colts driving for the go-ahead score, Johnny Unitas was hit by Willie Davis. He fumbled into the arms of Dave Robinson. Game over!

The Packers lost two games in 1966 by a total of four points. Bart Starr was tremendous with a league-leading completion percentage of 62%. He also threw just three interceptions in 251 attempts! Starr was the league's MVP in 1966, and he led the Packers to back-to-back titles.

⟫ NFL Championship Game 1/1/67
Packers @ Cowboys   Cotton Bowl   74,152

With the league's best record, the Packers were gunning for their second straight title when they met the Cowboys in Dallas. The winner would also represent the NFL in the first championship game against the AFL.

Both coaches, Vince Lombardi and Tom Landry, had worked together as assistant coaches for the Giants. Lombardi ran the offense, and Landry ran the defense. Because they knew one another well, they both changed plays and formations to keep things interesting. It worked, and nearly 800 total yards kept fans riveted.

Green Bay jumped in front 14-0 before Dallas even had the ball. Bart Starr found Elijah Pitts open out of the backfield for a 7-0 lead. On the ensuing kickoff, Mel Renfro fumbled, and Jim Grabowski ran it in for a 14-0 lead. The Cowboys bounced back to tie it before the end of the first quarter.

Bart Starr put the Packers back in front 21-14 with a beautiful touchdown pass to Carroll Dale. The defense then held the Cowboys to a field goal for a 21-17 halftime lead. Early in the third quarter, Elijah Pitts' fumble gave Dallas an opportunity. They drove to the Packer 32-yard line before having to settle for another field goal.

Starr followed the great play of the defense with a long drive that ended with a play-action touchdown pass to Boyd Dowler. Dowler injured his shoulder on the play from a late, upending hit in the end zone by Mike Gaechter.

With five minutes left and leading 28-20, Starr's fourth touchdown pass appeared to put the game out of reach. But Don Meredith roared back and threw a shocking 68-yard touchdown pass to Frank Clarke. On their next possession, the Packers couldn't move the ball, and Don Chandler's short punt gave Dallas the ball back at the Green Bay 47-yard line with 2:12 left.

The Cowboys moved to the Packer 22-yard line before a pass interference penalty on safety Tom Brown put the ball at the Green Bay two. An offside call against Cowboy tackle Jim Boeke moved the ball back to the six. Pettis Norman's clutch catch brought the ball back to the two yard line.

On fourth and goal from the one, Meredith rolled to his right. When Bob Hayes failed to block linebacker Dave Robinson, he chased and caught Meredith from behind. As Robinson took him down, *Dandy Don* threw a wobbly pass toward the back of the end zone that was intercepted by Tom Brown to clinch it.

Packers	14	7	7	6	34
Cowboys	14	3	3	7	27

⟩⟩ __Super Bowl I__ 1/15/67
Packers vs. Chiefs   L. A. Coliseum   61, 946

In one of most anticipated games in football history, the first Super Bowl matched the Packers of the NFL against the Chiefs of the AFL. Green Bay was a 13 point favorite, and 70 million television viewers watched it on two networks - CBS and NBC.

As champion of the older, more established league, the pressure was clearly on Green Bay. Lombardi knew how important the game was for the owners. A loss, or even a close game, would challenge the NFL's belief that it had the superior brand of football.

On the Packers' second possession, Bart Starr threw the first touchdown pass in Super Bowl history to Max McGee. It was the first of two touchdown catches for McGee who had replaced Boyd Dowler when he reinjured his shoulder on the third play of the game. But with their impressive size and speed, the Chiefs were quick to go 66 yards in five plays to tie things up.

The Packers struck back with a 73-yard drive capped off by a 14-yard *power sweep* by Jim Taylor. A Kansas City field goal cut the lead at half to 14-10, and the Chiefs proved they could play with Green Bay. They had sacked Starr twice, and outgained the Packers in the first half 181-164. The four point halftime lead was clearly not enough for Green Bay or the NFL.

At the end of the intermission, Lombardi challenged his team, "Are you the world champion Green Bay Packers?

Get on the field and give me your answer."12   The Packers knew they were in a battle, but they also knew what to do. They came out in the second half more aggressive on both sides, and it turned the game around. On a blitz, Dave Robinson deflected a Len Dawson pass and it was intercepted by Willie Wood. Wood returned it to the Chiefs five yard line, and Elijah Pitts scored on the next play.

In the third quarter, Starr then went right after cornerbacks Willie Mitchell and Fred Williamson. He made K. C. pay for playing eight men close to the line of scrimmage and challenging him to throw. He connected with McGee for another score, and his poise throughout the game, especially on third downs (10 for 14) tore the Chiefs' secondary to shreds.

Green Bay's defense had a fantastic day with six sacks. They held the Chiefs to 72 yards on the ground, and K. C. ran only four plays in Packer territory in the second half that resulted in one sack, two penalties and a punt. Elijah Pitts' two touchdowns in the second half put the game away.

Packers 7 7 14 7 35
Chiefs 0 10 0 0 10

"Kansas City has a good team. But they don't even rate with some of the teams in the NFL. Dallas is a better team. That's what you want me to say, isn't it? There. I've said it." 13

Vince Lombardi

1967 9-4-1
Offense # 9
Defense # 3

Green Bay had its sights set on winning three straight championships to match Curly Lambeau's three consecutive titles from 1929-1931. In 1967, every team in the league had its sights set on Green Bay. Beating the Packers salvaged the season for many teams, and the target on Green Bay's back could not have been bigger.

The season was challenging for the veteran Packers. They opened at home with a 17-17 tie with Detroit. After winning the next three, they lost to the Vikings in Milwaukee. The offense struggled for consistency without Taylor and Hornung, and Bart Starr missed 2+ games with a shoulder injury. His return against the Giants produced a 38 point second half that helped get the Packers back on track.

The Packers beat the Bears twice. The second win clinched the *new* Central Division of the Western Conference. It gave Green Bay the chance to defend its title, and play for three straight championships.

The season ended with losses to the Rams and last-place Pittsburgh. Though the 1967 Packers had the fewest regular season wins of Lombardi's championship teams, these veterans played the best when it counted the most. They hung together to bring home a third straight title to Green Bay.

⟩⟩ Western Conference Championship
12/23/67 Rams vs. Packers
Milwaukee County Stadium 49,861

When the Packers and the Rams met two weeks earlier in Los Angeles, the young Rams held their own against the veteran Packers. They outgained them by more than 100 yards, and won the game in the final minute 27-24. The Rams tied the Colts for the league's best record (11-1-2), and they were confident playing the Packers in the postseason.

On a cold day in Milwaukee (-3 wind chill), the Rams jumped right on Green Bay. In the first quarter, a fumble by Carroll Dale led to a Rams touchdown. The Packers got rolling in the second quarter when Travis Williams electrified the crowd with a 46-yard run for a touchdown! Green Bay scored again before halftime on a Bart Starr to Carroll Dale touchdown pass to lead 14-7.

While the Rams front four of Deacon Jones, Merlin Olson, Roger Brown, and Lamar Lundy was nationally known, the Green Bay line of Willie Davis, Henry Jordan, Ron Kostelnick, and Lionel Aldridge controlled the game. They shut down the Rams' high scoring offense by sacking quarterback Roman Gabriel five times (four by Henry Jordan).

In the second half, Starr orchestrated two long scoring drives to seal the deal. It was a great bounce back for Green Bay. Starr completed 17 of 23 passes, and the Packers outgained the Rams 374-217.

Rams	7	0	0	7	
Packers	0	14	7	7	28

➤ **NFL Championship Game** 12/31/67
Cowboys @ Packers Lambeau Field 50, 861

Minus 13 degrees. Minus 46 degrees wind chill. Brrrrr!! In one of the most famous games ever played, the Packers overcame extreme cold to become the first team since the 1929-31 Packers to win three straight NFL championships.

During the game, fans lit small fires inside the stadium to keep warm. The conditions were so brutal that an elderly man passed away. The cold shut down Lombardi's heating system under the field. When the tarpaulin was removed, the moisture under it fell to the ground and froze. Lombardi went ballistic, and the stage was set for the Ice Bowl.

Green Bay took an early lead took on two touchdown strikes from Bart Starr to Boyd Dowler. Two surprising turnovers by Bart Starr and Willie Wood let the Cowboys regroup. At halftime, Dallas trailed 14-10.

Dallas' *Doomsday Defense* pressured Starr all afternoon, and they sacked him eight times. In the third quarter, the Packers went scoreless, and the momentum began to shift. On the first play of the fourth quarter, the Cowboys grabbed the lead on a 50 yard halfback option pass from Dan Reeves to Lance Rentzel that stunned Green Bay. Dallas 17-14.

Both teams had trouble moving the ball after Dallas pulled in front. The Packers missed a 40-yard field goal with under 10 minutes left. When they got the ball back at their 32 yard line with 4:54 to go, they began their historic drive. Here's the 68-yard march that delivered Green Bay's third straight championship.

4:54	1-10-32	Starr 6 yard pass to Anderson
	2-4-38	Mercein runs for 7 yards-first down
	1-10-45	Starr 13 yard pass to Dowler-first down
	1-10-42	Anderson runs right, 9 yard loss
	2-19-49	Starr 12 yard pass to Anderson
	Two Minute Warning	
2:00	3-7-39	Starr 9 yard pass to Anderson
	1-10-30	Starr 19 yard pass to Mercein-first down
	1-10-11	Mercein runs for 8 yards
	Packer timeout	
:54	2-2-3	Anderson runs for 2 yards-first down
:30	1-goal-1	Anderson runs for no gain
	Packer timeout	
:20	2-goal-1	Anderson runs for no gain
	Packer timeout	
:16	3-goal-1	Starr sneaks in for TD (Chandler kick)

After the Ice Bowl, on his short ride home, Lombardi told his son Vince Jr., "You've just seen me coach my next to last game."[14] Many players thought about Lombardi's possible retirement, but first they had one more mountain to climb together – Super Bowl II, the final jewel of the Lombardi Dynasty.

Cowboys	0	10	0	7	17
Packers	7	7	0	7	21

You want to know the real reason we went for the touchdown instead of the field goal? Because I didn't want all those freezing people up in the stands to have to sit through a sudden death overtime. [15]

Vince Lombardi

➤ **Super Bowl II** **1/14/68**
Raiders vs. Packers   Orange Bowl   75,546

By the time the heavily favored Packers arrived in Miami, speculation about Lombardi's future was rampant. Many who knew him best believed this would be his last game, but Lombardi said nothing publicly.

The players had their suspicions, and during halftime, Jerry Kramer and a few veterans, "decided to play the last 30 minutes for the Old Man."[16]   They would give him a fine sendoff.

Similar to the first Super Bowl, the first half was close and competitive. Don Chandler started the scoring with two field goals. Bart Starr launched a beautiful 62-yard touchdown pass to Boyd Dowler to make it 13-0. Oakland then marched 78 yards to narrow the lead to 13-7 before the half.

The Packers came out of the locker room and whipped the Raiders by controlling the football for most of the third quarter. The second time they had the ball, Starr led a beautiful 82-yard touchdown drive. The key play was a classic third-and-one from the Packer 40-yard line. Starr faked to his fullback Ben Wilson, and hit Max McGee for a huge 35-yard gain. Seven plays later, Donny Anderson's two yard touchdown run capped the 11-play drive.

Defensively, Green Bay had an answer for everything. The Raiders had the ball for only nine plays in the third quarter, and they didn't score again until there was less than ten minutes left in the game. By then Willie Davis had three sacks, and Herb Adderley's 60 yard pick-six had made it 33-7. Fittingly, the final game of the Lombardi Dynasty was a dominant and resounding win!

Raiders	0	7	0	7	14
Packers	3	13	10	7	33

The Wolf Era
1991 – 200   95-52-0 (64%)
1 Championship

On January 12, 1969, the New York Jets became the first team from the American Football League to win the Super Bowl. They upset the heavily favored Baltimore Colts 16-7 in Super Bowl III. The Jets officially replaced the Packers as pro football's champion, and it wouldn't be until the 1996 season that the Packers would return to the big game. By that time, the trophy had been renamed to honor Vince Lombardi.

The Packer franchise first began to reawaken when Bob Harlan was appointed President in 1989. Harlan had worked for the Packers since 1971, and he ignited the turnaround by hiring Ron Wolf to direct football operations in 1991. Wolf hired Mike Holmgren, traded for Brett Favre, and signed free agent Reggie White to set a new direction for the franchise.

Green Bay was back in the postseason after two years. In Wolf's fifth season, they won the Super Bowl. Though they returned the Super Bowl the following season, they did not repeat. Wolf kept the Packers' cupboard well-stocked through trades, the draft, and free agency acquisitions. Following his retirement, the winning has continued and expectations for the Packers have remained at the highest level.

1996 13-3-0
Offense # 1
Defense # 1

After losing to Dallas in the conference championship game in 1995, the Packers were primed for another shot at the Super Bowl. They had the league's best offense and defense, and a pledge* from their quarterback in training camp to lead the franchise back to the big game.

The season got off to a great start. They clobbered the Buccaneers, Eagles and Chargers by a combined score of 115-26. Their first loss came in the Twin Cities where Favre was sacked seven times, and the offense was held to eight first downs. It was their sixth straight loss in the Metrodome.

Five straight wins followed, including a Monday Night overtime thriller against San Francisco. Unfortunately for Green Bay, Robert Brooks tore his ACL in the game and was lost for the season. Two weeks later, Antonio Freeman broke his left forearm and missed four games. Tight end Mark Chmura tore an arch in his foot and missed three games. After losing to the Chiefs and the Cowboys, Green Bay signed free agent wide receiver Andrea Rison to give Favre another weapon in the passing game.

* *At his press conference on July 17 1996, after 46 days at the Menninger Clinic in Topeka, Kansas, Brett Favre promised to lead the Packers to the Super Bowl.*

The Packers got back on track and won eight straight. In the last six games of the season, they scored an average of 35 points a game while giving up just nine. They beat the Bears for a sixth straight time, and the running game found its stride. They were ready for the NFC's #1 postseason seed.

▷ NFC Divisional Playoff 1/4/97
49ers @ Packers   Lambeau Field   60,787

The *muddy* tundra of Lambeau Field couldn't slow down the determined Packers who ran the ball 39 times for 139 yards. They plowed ahead while the 49ers suffered injuries to quarterback Steve Young and defensive tackle Bryant Young. Backup quarterback Elvis Grbac couldn't fill Young's shoes, and the defense couldn't contain the Packers.

On the fifth play of the game, seven 49ers missed Desmond Howard on his way to a 71-yard punt return to start the scoring. A short time later, Howard's 46-yard return set up Brett Favre's short touchdown pass to Andrea Rison. The defense struck the next blow with Craig Newsome's interception. It led to Green Bay's third touchdown and a 21-0 lead.

San Francisco came back. A muffed punt by Green Bay late in the second quarter gave the 49ers the ball at the Green Bay 26. Six plays later, an eight yard touchdown pass to Terry Kirby cut the Packer halftime lead to 21-7.

Immediately after the break, San Francisco's resurgence continued. When Desmond Howard did not get back on the field in time for the second half kickoff, a rattled Don Beebe let the kickoff bounce past him. It was recovered by Steve Israel at the Packer four yard line. On the next play, Grbac ran it in for a 21-14 game.

With their lead vanishing, the Packers regrouped. On their next drive, they ran the ball in the mud doggedly and effectively ten times. The march ended on an Edgar Bennett fumble that was fortunately recovered by Antonio Freeman in the end zone for a 28-14 lead.

Green Bay's #1 defense dug in and grabbed three picks and recovered two fumbles. The fumble recoveries came late in the fourth quarter, locking up a spot for Green Bay in the NFC Championship Game.

49ers	0	7	7	0	14
Packers	14	7	7	7	35

❯ NFC Championship Game 1/12 /97
Panthers @ Packers   Lambeau Field   60,216

Sunny skies couldn't disguise the bitter cold for the most important game at Lambeau Field since the Ice Bowl. The game time temperature of 3 degrees (-17 wind chills) was a bit uncomfortable for the team from North Carolina.

The mercurial Andrea Rison gave a fiery pre-game speech for the Packers, but Brett Favre got off to a rocky start. He threw an interception that led to a quick 7-0 Carolina lead. He then righted the ship with a second quarter touchdown pass to Dorsey Levens, unfortunately his fumble later in the quarter led to a Carolina field goal.

Favre shook off the inconsistent start, and the Packer defense allowed only three points the rest of the way. Favre orchestrated four scoring drives of 70 yards or more, and Levens had his best game as a Packer with 88 yards rushing and 117 receiving. His catch of Favre's amazing shovel pass as he was being tackled by two Carolina defenders was one the game's most spectacular plays.

At the end of the third quarter, Levens romped 66 yards on a screen pass to set up Edgar Bennett's touchdown to put the game away. Green Bay's defense had no trouble with the Panthers. They sacked Kerry Collins twice, picked off two passes, and held Carolina to 45 yards on the ground. Green Bay was now Super Bowl bound!

$$\begin{array}{lccccc} \textbf{Panthers} & \textbf{7} & \textbf{3} & \textbf{3} & \textbf{0} & \textbf{13} \\ \textbf{Packers} & \textbf{0} & \textbf{17} & \textbf{10} & \textbf{3} & \textbf{30} \end{array}$$

Congratulations, you deserve this. [17]
Brett Favre to Reggie White

 ## Super Bowl XXXI 1/26/97
Patriots vs. Packers   Superdome   75,546

The Green Bay Packers returned to the Super Bowl for the first time since 1968. They brought with them the NFL's #1 offense and defense, and one of the game's top young quarterbacks, Brett Favre, from nearby Kiln, Mississippi.

The game couldn't t have started any better for the Packers. On their second play from scrimmage, Favre detected a blitz and called an audible. He connected on a post pattern with Andrea Rison for a 54-yard touchdown. Doug Evans picked-off Drew Bledsoe, and Chris Jacke converted a 37-yard field goal for an early 10-0 lead.

New England brushed off the bad start, and came with an aggressive passing attack that surprised Green Bay. Two touchdown drives put the Patriots in front 14-10. The Packers reclaimed the lead quickly when Favre spotted press coverage on Antonio Freeman and hit him in stride for an 81 yard touchdown. Another field goal, and Favre's short touchdown run made it 27-14 at half.

Green Bay's offense slowed down in the second half, but the defense remained stout. They had five sacks, two coming on Reggie White's consecutive sacks in the third quarter. They picked off four passes (three in the second half), and allowed only 43 yards on the ground all game. Eighteen of those yards came on Curtis Martin's run up the middle to make it 27-21. The momentum shifted slightly.

Desmond Howard took it all back by going 99 yards on the ensuing kickoff. The two-point conversion made it a two touchdown lead entering the fourth quarter. When Reggie White sacked Bledsoe with 1:49 left, it was over. MVP honors went to Desmond Howard who had returned six punts and four kickoffs for 244 yards! The Packers finished with the most wins in franchise history (16-3), and they were Super Bowl Champions for the first time in 28 years!

Patriots	**14**	**0**	**7**	**0**	**21**
Packers	**10**	**17**	**8**	**0**	**35**

The Thompson Era
2005 - 108-67-1 (61%)
1 Championship

When Ron Wolf retired in 2001, Head Coach Mike Sherman was given the additional title of General Manager which added player personnel to his responsibilities. After four years, Bob Harlan decided to separate the positions of Coach and General Manager. Harlan brought back Ted Thompson from Seattle in 2005 to handle the General Manager duties. Thompson had previously worked in the Packer personnel department under Ron Wolf.

Mike Sherman remained as coach. But after a disastrous 4-12 season in 2005, Thompson replaced Sherman with Mike McCarthy, the offensive coordinator of the San Francisco 49ers. Sherman's record was 59-43-0 in six seasons, and the Packers made the postseason four times.

Since 2006, Mike McCarthy's record has been 104-65-1. He has led the Packers to the postseason eight times, and won Super Bowl XLV.

2010 10-6-0
Offense # 10
Defense # 2

Though they were one of the favorites to win the Super Bowl, the Packers started slowly. They built-up steam during the regular season despite placing 14 players on season ending Injured Reserve (IR). Three others missed seven games on the Physically Unable to Perform list (PUP).

A nice road win over Michael Vick and the Eagles started the season. They soundly defeated Buffalo at home before losing to the Bears on a last second field goal. After beating Detroit, they lost two straight overtime games for a mediocre 3-3 record.

A four game winning streak was framed by two wins over Minnesota. In between they slaughtered the Jets and Cowboys by a combined score of 54-7.

In December, Aaron Rodgers suffered a concussion in the second quarter against the Lions and missed the rest of the game. He had to sit out the next game against New England. The Packers lost both games. To make the postseason, Green Bay needed to win its last two games against New York and Chicago. They succeeded, and captured the sixth and final seed in the NFC playoffs.

⟩⟩ __NFC Wild Card__ 1/9/11
Packers @ Eagles   Lincoln Financial Field   69,144

In 1960, the Packers lost to the Eagles in the NFL Championship Game. Other than a 1964 loss to the Cardinals in the old *Playoff Bowl*, this was the only postseason loss of the Lombardi Dynasty.

Unlike Green Bay, Philadelphia stumbled into the postseason with two straight losses. Green Bay hoped to continue the trend, with a 68-yard touchdown drive to open the scoring. A James Jones touchdown catch made it 14-0. Just before halftime, David Akers got the Eagles on the board with a 29-yard field goal.

An Aaron Rodgers fumble at the start of the second half allowed the Eagles to cut the lead to 14-10. For the next seven minutes, Rodgers and rookie running back James Starks led the Packers on an impressive drive. Rodgers found Brandon Jackson for his third touchdown pass and the Packers led 21-10.

In the fourth quarter, a determined Michael Vick led a 12-play drive that brought the Eagles to the Packer one yard line. On fourth and goal, Vick took it in himself to trim the lead to 21-16 with four minutes left. When Green Bay did little on their next drive, Philadelphia got the ball back with 1:45 left.

In five plays, the Eagles moved from their 34 yard line to the Packers' 27. With 44 seconds left, Vick lofted a first-down pass to 6'3" Riley Cooper in the end zone. Tramon Williams, Green Bay's 5'11" cornerback, went up and intercepted the pass. In the jubilant locker room after the game, Williams pointed out, "I'm 5-11, but I can jump, too."[18]

The Packer defense had a great day. They held Vick to 32 yards rushing, and they limited his number of big plays. On offense, Rodgers and Starks gave Green Bay an unexpected balance. Starks' 123 yards on the ground broke Travis Williams' rookie postseason record of 88 yards rushing against the Rams in 1967.

Packers	7	7	7	0	21
Eagles	0	3	7	6	16

NFC Divisional Playoff 1/15/11
Packers @ Falcons   Georgia Dome   69,210

The Packers returned to the Georgia Dome to meet the NFC's #1 seed – the Falcons. In November, Green Bay lost to Atlanta in the final seconds on a 47-yard field goal.

The rematch didn't start well for the Packers when Greg Jennings fumbled at midfield. Atlanta recovered and capitalized seven plays later for a 7-0 lead. Green Bay came right back with an impressive 14 play drive that was capped off with a six yard touchdown pass to Jordy Nelson. Atlanta punched right back on the ensuing kickoff when Eric Weems darted right up the middle for a 102 yard return.

Rodgers and the Packers responded by marching 92 yards to tie it at 14 on John Kuhn's one yard plunge over right tackle. With 2:30 left before halftime, the game changed dramatically. Tramon Williams intercepted the first of two Matt Ryan passes. The first led to an 80 yard touchdown drive, and the second, with 10 seconds left in the half, was a 70 yard pick-six to make it 28-14!

Rodgers and Starks drove the Packers downfield for another touchdown to put the game away in the third quarter. This time around, the Packers had outgained the Falcons by more than 200 yards, and the 48 points scored was a Green Bay postseason record. Rodgers led five straight scoring drives for a stellar performance (31-36-366-3-0). Along with a defense that took the ball away four times and recorded five sacks, it was total domination.

Packers	0	28	14	6	48
Falcons	7	7	0	7	21

 ## NFC Championship Game 1/23/11
Packers @ Bears   Soldier Field   62,377

After splitting their two games in 2010, the Packers and the Bears played the most important game in their storied history. The stakes could not have been higher - Super Bowl XLV!

Aaron Rodgers got things rolling for Green Bay on their opening possession with an 84 yard touchdown march. They stretched the lead to 14 early in the second quarter when James Starks took it around right end for another score. On both drives, Rodgers completed every pass and the Packers were in control.

After one series in the second half, Bears' quarterback Jay Cutler left the game with a knee injury. He was replaced by Todd Collins. On Green Bay's first possession of the second half, they were in position to deliver the knockout punch

from the Chicago six yard line. But linebacker Brian Urlacher picked off Rodgers' pass, and took off with only Rodgers to beat. After a 40-yard chase, Rodgers brought him down at the Bears' 45-yard line. The tackle saved a touchdown, and the Bears went three and out.

Backup quarterback Todd Collins was ineffective. He did not complete a pass, and was replaced by Caleb Hanie late in the third quarter. Hanie re-energized the Bears with a quick drive to cut the Packer advantage to 14-7 with 11 minutes left. Five minutes later, Packer defensive tackle B.J. Raji squashed any talk of a Bears comeback when he stepped off the line toward the flat and intercepted a pass at the 18 yard line. He returned it for a big touchdown, a big dance, and a 21-7 Packer lead.

On the next drive, Hanie remained poised and connected on four straight passes leading to a touchdown. When the Packers went three-and-out on their next series, Chicago got the ball back at their 29-yard line with under three minutes to play. On the twelfth play of the drive, Sam Shields stole his second pass of the day with 47 seconds left. It finished off *Da Bears,* and the Packers were off to the Super Bowl!

Packers	7	7	0	7	21
Bears	0	0	0	14	14

⟫ **Super Bowl XLV** 2/6/11
Steelers vs. Packers   Cowboys Stadium   103,219

Green Bay was the first sixth seeded team from the NFC to ever reach the Super Bowl. In 2005, the Steelers did the same in the AFC. In 2010, both teams brought deep traditions, great quarterbacks, strong defenses, and great fans to the big game.

Turnovers played a huge role in this Super Bowl, and the Packers cashed in three times. After Aaron Rodgers and Jordy Nelson connected for a first quarter touchdown, the turnovers took center stage. On the Steelers next possession, defensive tackle Howard Green hit Ben Roethlisberger's arm just as he released his pass. Nick Collins caught the wounded duck, and returned it 37 yards for a 14-0 Packer lead. With two minutes left in the half, the Packers capitalized on another interception to make it 21-3 on a bullet from Rodgers to Greg Jennings.

Though It was beginning to look like a blowout, Roethlisberger rallied the Steelers before the break. He went five-for-seven on the next drive, and moved the Steelers to the Packer eight yard line. Hines Ward caught the touchdown pass to cut the lead to 21-10. The Packers led at halftime, but they would have to play the second half without two of their injured stars - Donald Driver and Charles Woodson.

The second half started out perfectly for Pittsburgh. After picking up one first down, Green Bay punted. A face mask penalty against the Packers put the ball at midfield. Five minutes later, Rashard Mendenhall scored from the eight yard line and the Steelers had cut the lead to four.

The game's pivotal moment came on the first play of the final quarter. On a crushing hit by Clay Matthews and Ryan Pickett, Mendenhall coughed up the ball, and Desmond Bishop recovered for the Packers. In three minutes, Rodgers had the Packers in the end zone on a pass to Jennings for a 28-17 lead.

Roethlisberger countered quickly with eight straight passes. He hit Mike Wallace from 25 yards out for the score, and the two-point conversion cut the Packer lead to 28-25 with 7:40 left. The momentum was now with the Steel City.

After picking up three first downs, Green Bay's drive stalled. Mason Crosby's field goal stretched the lead to six (31-25) with two minutes left. It was up Green Bay's #2 defense, minus Charles Woodson, to protect a six point lead against a Hall of Fame quarterback competing for his third Super Bowl Ring. Roethlisberger picked up one first down, but three incompletions ended the game. The Packers, who persevered through injuries all season, won the big game once again behind the strong and accurate arm of Aaron Rodgers, Super Bowl XLV MVP.

Steelers	0	10	7	8	25
Packers	14	7	0	10	31

Rare is it when a legend leaves and his successor is up to the task of replacing him. [19]

Peter King

APPENDIX

1929

	W	L	T	%	PF	PA
Green Bay	12	0	1	1.000	198	22
New York	13	1	1	.929	312	86
Frankford	9	4	5	.692	129	128
Chicago Cards.	6	6	1	.500	154	83
Boston	4	4	0	.500	98	73
Orange	3	4	4	.429	35	80
Staten Island	3	4	3	.429	89	65
Providence	4	6	2	.400	107	117
Chicago Bears	4	9	2	.308	119	227
Buffalo	1	7	1	.125	48	142
Minneapolis	1	9	0	.100	48	185
Dayton	0	6	0	.000	7	136

Packers vs. Giants

Packers 7 0 0 13   20
Giants   0 0 6   0   6
GB   McCreary 3yd pass from Lewellen (Molenda kick)
NY   Plansky 38yd pass from Friedman (kick failed)
GB   Molenda 1yd run (Molenda kick)
GB   Blood 5yd run (Molenda kick)

1930

	W	L	T	%	PF	PA
Green Bay	10	3	1	.769	234	111
New York	13	4	0	.765	308	96
Chicago Bears	9	4	1	.692	169	71
Brooklyn	7	4	1	.636	154	59
Providence	6	4	1	.600	90	125
Staten Island	5	5	2	.500	95	112
Chicago Cards.	5	6	2	.455	128	132
Portsmouth	5	6	3	.455	176	161
Frankford	4	13	1	.222	113	321
Minneapolis	1	7	1	.125	27	165
Newark	1	10	1	.091	51	190

Packers vs. Portsmouth Spartans

Packers   6 0 0 0 6
Spartans 0 6 0 0 6
GB   Engelemann 15yd pass from Dunn (kick failed)
PT   Bennett 8yd run (kick failed)

1931

	W	L	T	%	PF	PA
Green Bay	12	2	0	.857	291	87
Portsmouth	11	3	0	.786	175	77
Chicago Bears	8	5	0	.615	145	92
Chicago Cards.	5	4	0	.556	120	128
New York	7	6	1	.538	154	100
Providence	4	4	3	.500	78	127
Staten Island	4	6	1	.400	79	118
Cleveland	2	8	0	.200	45	137
Brooklyn	2	12	0	.143	64	199
Frankford	1	6	1	.143	13	99

Providence Steam Roller vs. Packers

Steam Roller	0	7	13	0	20
Packers	21	7	0	20	48

GB   Engelmann 29yd pass from Dunn (Dunn kick)
GB   Engelmann 32yd pass from Dunn (Dunn kick)
GB   Engelmann 85yd kickoff return (Dunn kick)
PR   Pape 1yd run (Shelley kick)
GB   Dilweg on a lateral from Blood/pass from Grove (Grove kick)
PR   Pape 10yd pass from Shelley (kick failed)
PR   Pape 6yd pass from Shelley (Shelley kick)
GB   Wilson 45yd run (kick failed)
GB   Molenda 4yd run (Molenda kick)
GB   Grove 40yd pass from Molenda (Molenda kick)

1936

Western Division	W	L	T	%	PF	PA
Green Bay	10	1	1	.909	248	118
Chicago Bears	9	3	0	.750	222	94
Detroit	8	4	0	.667	235	102
Chicago Cards.	3	8	1	.273	74	143

Eastern Division	W	L	T	%	PF	PA
Boston	7	5	0	.583	149	110
Pittsburgh	6	6	0	.500	98	187
New York	5	6	1	.455	115	163
Brooklyn	3	8	1	.273	92	161
Philadelphia	1	11	0	.083	51	206

1936 NFL Championship Game

Packers	7	0	7	7	21
Redskins	0	6	0	0	6

GB   Hutson 43yd pass from Herber (Smith kick)
BR   Rentner 1yd run (kick failed)
GB   Gantenbein 8yd pass from Herber (Smith kick)
GB   Monnett 2yd run (Engebretsen)

1939

Western Division	W	L	T	%	PF	PA
Green Bay	9	2	0	.818	233	153
Chicago Bears	8	3	0	.727	298	157
Detroit	6	5	0	.545	145	150
Cleveland	5	5	1	.500	195	164
Chicago Cards.	1	10	1	.091	84	254

Eastern Division	W	L	T	%	PF	PA
New York	9	1	1	.900	168	85
Washington	8	2	1	.800	242	92
Brooklyn	4	6	1	.400	108	219
Philadelphia	1	9	1	.100	105	200
Pittsburgh	1	9	1	.100	114	216

1939 NFL Championship Game

Giants 0 0 0 0 0
Packers 7 0 10 10 27
GB Gantenbein 7yd pass from Herber (Engebretsen kick)
GB Engebretsen 29yd FG
GB Laws 31yd pass from Isbell (Engebretsen kick)
GB Smith 42yd FG
GB Jankowski 1yd run (Smith kick)

1944

Western Division	W	L	T	%	PF	PA
Green Bay	8	2	0	.800	238	141
Chicago Bears	6	3	1	.667	258	172
Detroit	6	3	1	.667	216	151
Cleveland	4	6	0	.400	188	244
Card-Pitt	0	10	0	.000	108	228

Eastern Division	W	L	T	%	PF	PA
New York	8	1	1	.889	206	75
Philadelphia	7	1	2	.875	267	131
Washington	6	3	1	.667	169	180
Boston	2	8	0	.200	82	233
Brooklyn	0	10	0	.000	69	166

1944 NFL Championship Game

Packers 0 14 0 0   14
Giants   0   0 0 0   0

GB   Fritsch 1yd run (Hutson kick)
GB   Fritsch 28yd pass from Comp (Hutson kick)
NY   Cuff 1yd run (Strong kick)

1961

Western Division	W	L	T	%	PF	PA
Green Bay	11	3	0	.786	391	223
Detroit	8	5	1	.615	270	258
Baltimore	8	6	0	.571	302	307
Chicago	8	6	0	.571	326	302
San Francisco	7	6	1	.538	346	272
Los Angeles	4	10	0	.286	263	333
Minnesota	3	11	0	.214	285	407

Eastern Division	W	L	T	%	PF	PA
New York	10	3	1	.769	368	220
Philadelphia	10	4	0	.714	361	297
Cleveland	8	5	1	.615	319	270
St. Louis	7	7	0	.500	279	267
Pittsburgh	6	8	0	.429	295	287
Dallas	4	9	1	.308	236	380
Washington	1	12	1	.077	174	392

1961 NFL Championship Game

Giants	0	0	0	0	0
Packers	0	24	10	3	37

GB Horning 6yd run (Hornung kick)
GB Dowler 13yd pass from Starr (Hornung kick)
GB Kramer 14yd pass from Starr (Hornung kick)
GB Hornung 17yd FG
GB Hornung 22yd FG
GB Kramer 13yd pass from Starr
GB Hornung 19yd FG

1962

Western Division	W	L	T	%	PF	PA
Green Bay	13	1	0	.929	415	148
Detroit	11	3	0	.786	315	177
Chicago	9	5	0	.643	321	287
Baltimore	7	7	0	.500	293	288
San Francisco	6	8	0	.429	346	272
Minnesota	2	11	1	.154	254	410
Los Angeles	1	12	1	.077	220	334

Eastern Division	W	L	T	%	PF	PA
New York	12	2	0	.857	398	283
Pittsburgh	9	5	0	.643	312	363
Cleveland	7	6	1	.538	291	257
Washington	5	7	2	.417	305	376
Dallas	5	8	1	.385	398	402
St. Louis	4	9	1	.308	287	361
Philadelphia	3	10	1	.231	282	356

1962 NFL Championship Game

Packers	3	7	3	3	16
Giants	0	0	7	0	7

GB   J. Kramer 26yd FG
GB   Taylor 7yd run (J. Kramer kick)
NY   Collier punt recovery TD (Chandler kick)
GB   J. Kramer 29yd FG
GB   J. Kramer 30yd FG

1965

Western Division	W	L	T	%	PF	PA
Green Bay	10	3	1	.769	316	224
Baltimore	10	3	1	.769	389	284
Chicago	9	5	0	.643	409	275
San Francisco	7	6	1	.538	421	402
Minnesota	7	7	0	.500	383	403
Detroit	6	7	1	.462	257	295
Los Angeles	4	10	1	.286	269	328

Eastern Division	W	L	T	%	PF	PA
Cleveland	11	3	0	.786	363	325
Dallas	7	7	0	.500	325	280
New York	7	7	0	.538	270	338
Washington	6	8	0	.429	257	301
Philadelphia	5	9	0	.357	363	359
St. Louis	5	9	0	.357	296	309
Philadelphia	2	12	0	.143	202	397

1965 Western Conference Playoff

```
Colts    7 3 0 0  0  10
Packers  0 0 7 3  3  13
```

BA Shinnick 25yd fumble return (Michaels kick)
BA Michaels 15yd FG
GB Hornung 1yd run
GB Chandler 22yd FG   (OT) GB Chandler 22yd FG

1965 NFL Championship Game

```
Browns  9 3 0 0  12
Packers 7 6 7 3  23
```

GB Dale (Chandler kick)
CL Collins 17yd pass from Ryan (kick failed)
CL Groza 24yd FG
GB Chandler 15yd FG
GB Chandler 23yd FG
CL Groza 28yd FG
GB Hornung 13yd run (Chandler kick)
GB Chandler 29yd FG

1966

Western Division	W	L	T	%	PF	PA
Green Bay	12	2	0	.857	335	163
Baltimore	9	5	0	.643	314	226
Los Angeles	8	6	0	.571	289	212
San Francisco	6	6	2	.500	320	325
Chicago	5	7	2	.417	234	272
Detroit	4	9	1	.308	206	317
Los Angeles	4	9	1	.308	292	304

Eastern Division	W	L	T	%	PF	PA
Dallas	10	3	1	.769	445	239
Cleveland	9	5	0	.643	403	259
Philadelphia	9	5	0	.643	326	340
St. Louis	8	5	1	.615	264	265
Washington	7	7	0	.500	351	355
Pittsburgh	5	8	1	.385	316	347
Atlanta	3	11	0	.214	204	437
New York	1	12	1	.077	263	501

1966 NFL Championship Game

Packers 14 7 7 6   34
Cowboys 14 3   3 7   27

GB   Pitts 17yd pass from Starr (Chandler kick)
GB   Grabowski 18yd fumble return (Chandler kick)
DA   Reeves 3yd run (Villanueva kick)
DA   Perkins 23yd run (Villanueva kick)
GB   Dale 51yd pass from Starr (Chandler kick)
DA   Villanueva 11yd FG
DA   Villanueva 32yd FG
GB   Dowler 16yd pass from Starr (Chandler kick)
GB   McGee 28yd pass from Starr (kick failed)
DA   Clarke 68yd pass from Meredith

Super Bowl I

Packers 7 7 14 7 35
Chiefs 0 10 0 0 10
GB McGee 37yd pass from Starr
KC McClinton 7yd pass from Dawson (Mercer kick)
GB Taylor 14yd run (Chandler kick)
KC Mercer 31yd FG
GB Pitts 5yd run (Chandler kick)
GB McGee 13yd pass from Starr (Chandler kick)
GB Pitts 1yd run (Chandler kick)

1967

Western Conference - Central Division

	W	L	T	%	PF	PA
Green Bay	9	4	1	.692	332	209
Chicago	7	6	1	.538	239	218
Detroit	5	7	2	.417	260	259
Minnesota	3	8	3	.273	233	294

Eastern Conference - Capitol Division

	W	L	T	%	PF	PA
Dallas	9	5	0	.643	342	268
Philadelphia	6	7	1	.462	351	409
Washington	5	6	3	.455	347	353
New Orleans	3	11	0	.214	233	379

Western Conference Playoff Game

Rams   7 0 0 0 7
Packers 0 14 7 7 28
LA Casey 29yd pass from Gabriel (Gossett kick)
GB Williams 46yd run (Chandler kick)
GB Dale 17yd pass from Starr (Chandler kick)
GB Mercein 6yd run (Chandler kick)
GB Williams 2yd run (Chandler kick)

NFL Championship Game

```
Cowboys  0  10  0  7   17
Packers  7   7  0  7   21
```

GB Dowler 8yd pass from Starr (Chandler kick)
GB Dowler 43yd pass from Starr (Chandler kick)
DA Andrie 7yd fumble return (Villanueva kick)
DA Villaneueva 21yd FG
DA Rentzel 50yd pass from Reeves (Villanueva kick)
GB Starr 1yd run (Chandler kick)

Super Bowl II

```
Packers  3  13  10  7   33
Raiders  0   7   0  7   14
```

GB Chandler 39yd FG
GB Chandler 20yd FG
GB Dowler 62yd pass from Starr (Chandler kick)
OK Miller 23yd pass from Lamonica (Blanda kick)
GB Chandler 43yd FG
GB Anderson 2yd run (Chandler kick)
GB Chandler 31yd FG
GB Adderley 60yd interception return (Chandler kick)
OA Miller 23yd pass from Lamonica (Blanda kick)

1996

National Conference - Central Division

	W	L	T	%	PF	PA
Green Bay	13	3	0	.813	456	210
Minnesota	9	7	0	.563	298	315
Chicago	7	9	0	.438	283	305
Tampa Bay	6	10	0	.375	221	293
Detroit	5	11	0	.313	302	368

American Conference - Eastern Division

	W	L	T	%	PF	PA
New England	11	5	0	.688	418	313
Buffalo	10	6	0	.625	319	266
Indianapolis	9	7	0	.563	317	334
Miami	8	8	0	.500	339	325
New York	1	15	0	.063	279	454

NFC Divisional Playoff

```
49ers    0  7  7  0  14
Packers 14  7  7  7  35
```

GB Howard 71yd punt return (Jacke kick)
GB Rison 4yd pass from Favre (Jacke kick)
GB Bennett 2yd run (Jacke kick)
SF Kirby 8yd pass from Grbac (Wilkins kick)
SF Grbac 4yd run (Wilkins kick)
GB Freeman fumble recovery in end zone (Jacke kick)
GB Bennett 11yd run (Jacke kick)

NFC Championship Game

```
Panthers 7  3  3  0  13
Packers  0 17 10  3  30
```

CA Griffith 3yd pass from Collins (Kasay kick)
GB Levens 29yd pass from Favre (Jacke kick)
CA Kasay 22yd FG
GB Freeman 6yd pass from Favre
GB Jacke 31yd FG
GB Jacke 32yd FG
CA Kasay 23yd FG
GB Bennett 4yd run (Jacke kick)
GB Jacke 28yd FG

Super Bowl XXXI

```
Patriots 7  0  7  7  21
Packers 10 17  8  0  35
```

GB Rison 54ydpass from Favre (Jacke kick)
GB Jacke 37yd FG
NE Byars 1yd pass from Bledsoe (Vinatieri kick)
NE Coates 4yd pass from Bledsoe (Vinatieri kick)
GB Freeman 81yd pass (Jacke kick)
GB Jacke 31yd FG
GB Favre 2yd run (Jacke kick)
NE Martin 18yd run (Vinatieri kick)
GB Howard 99yd kickoff return (2pt conversion)

2010

National Conference – North Division

	W	L	T	%	PF	PA
Chicago	11	5	0	.688	334	286
Green Bay	10	6	0	.625	388	240
Minnesota	6	10	0	.375	362	369
Tampa Bay	6	10	0	.375	281	348

American Conference – North Division

	W	L	T	%	PF	PA
Pittsburgh	12	4	0	.750	375	232
Baltimore	12	4	0	.750	357	270
Cleveland	5	11	0	.313	271	332
Cincinnati	4	12	0	.250	322	39

Wild Card Game

Packers 7 7 7 0 21
Eagles   0 3 7 6 16
GB   Crabtree 7yd pass from Rodgers (Crosby kick)
GB   Jones 9yd pass from Rodgers (Crosby kick)
PH   Akers 29yd FG
PH   Avant 24yd pass from Vick (Akers kick)
GB   Jackson 16yd pass from Rodgers (Crosby kick)
PH   Vick 1yd run (pass failed)

NFC Divisional Playoff

Packers 0 28 14 6 48
Falcons 7 7   0   7 21
ATL   Turner 12yd run (Bryant kick)
GB   Nelson 6y pass from Rodgers (Crosby kick)
ATL   Weems 102yd kickoff return (Bryant kick)
GB   Kuhn 1yd run (Crosby kick)
GB   Jones 29yd pass from Rodgers (Crosby kick)
GB   Williams 70 interception return (Crosby kick)
GB   Rodgers 7yd run (Crosby kick)
GB   Kuhn 7yd pass from Rodgers (Crosby kick)
ATL   White 6yd pass from Ryan (Bryant kick)
GB   Crosby 43yd FG
GB   Crosby 23yd FG

NFC Championship Game

Packers 7 7 0 7   21
Bears   0 0 0 14   14

GB   Rodgers 1yd run (Crosby kick)
GB   Starks 4yd run (Crosby kick)
CHI Taylor 1yd run (Gould kick)
GB   Raji 18yd interception return
CHI Bennett 35yd pass from Hanie (Gould kick)

Super Bowl XLV

Steelers 0 10 7 8   25
Packers   14 7 0 10   31

GB   Nelson 29yd pass from Rodgers (Crosby kick)
GB   Collins 37yd interception return (Crosby kick)
PG   Suisham 33yd FG
GB   Jennings 21yd pass from Rodgers (Crosby kick)
PG   Ward 8yd pass from Roethlisberger (Suisham kick)
PG   Mendenhall 8yd run (Suisham kick)
GB   Jennings 8yd pass from Rodgers (Crosby kick)
PG   Wallace 25yd pass from Roethlisberger (Randle El run)
GB   Crosby 23yd FG

giantcheeseheads.com

Notes

1929
1. packerhistory.net/1929Packers
2. Art Daley, New York Times, 11/25/1929

1930
3. Pigskin: The Early Years of Football, p. 115
4. packerhistory.net/1930

1936
5. Green Bay Press Gazette, 12/14/1936

1939
6. goldenrankings.com/NFLChampionshipGame1939
7. Green Bay Press Gazette, 12/11/1939

1944
8. goldenrankings.com/NFLChampionshipGame1944

1961
9. Lombardi, John Wiebusch, p. 118
10. Magnificent Seven, Bud Lea, p.22

1962
11. Y.A. Tittle: I Pass!, Don Smith, p. 238

1966
12. Greatest Football Games of All-Time, H. Hersch, p.20
13. Magnificent Seven, Bud Lea, p. 128

1967
14. When Pride Still Mattered, Dave Maraniss, p. 427
15. Sporting News, January 13, 1968, p.3
16. Magnificent Seven, Bud Lea, p.177

1996
17. Return to Glory, Kevin Isaacson, p. 187

2010
18. Milwaukee Journal Sentinel, 1/10/2011, p.3c
19. Sports Illustrated, 1/31/2011

Books

A Measure of Greatness, Eric Goska
Championship, Jerry Izenberg
Giants Among Men, Ernie Palladino
Greatest Football Games of All Time, Hank Hersch
Green Bay Packers: Trails, Triumphs and Tradition, W. Povletich
Ice Bowl, Ed Gruver
Lambeau, David Zimmerman
Lombardi, John Wiebusch
Magnificent Seven, Bud Lea
Pigskin: The Early Years of Football, Robert Peterson
The Packer Legend, John Torinus
Y.A. Tittle: I Pass!
When Pride Still Mattered, David Maraniss

Websites

goldenrankings.com
packershistory.net
pro-footballreference.com

Periodicals

Chicago Tribune
Green Bay Press Gazette
Milwaukee Journal/Sentinel
New York Times
New York Daily News
Sporting News
Sports Illustrated

giantcheeseheads.com